DEAR BABY:

I'm SORRY...

Apologies for Life's Little Parenting Fails

SARAH SHOWFETY

 sourcebooks

Published by Sourcebooks, Inc.
P.O. Box 4410, Naperville, Illinois 60567–4410
(630) 961–3900
Fax: (630) 961–2168
www.sourcebooks.com

Printed and bound in China.
LEO 10 9 8 7 6 5 4 3 2 1

#ParentingFail

DEAR BABY: Sorry I left you home alone with Daddy the day after taco night.

DEAR BABY: Sorry, this is pretty much all that's coming through the boob canal tonight.

DEAR BABY: Sorry, we may have rushed into this.

DEAR BABY: Sorry these are my New Year's resolutions.

Resolutions

1) clip baby's nails without drawing blood
2) sex with hubs once per quarter
3) brush teeth before noon
4) hate daddy less for being able to leave the house alone
5) bi-weekly shower
6) find out who the hell Peppa Pig is
7) go a day without Milano cookies
8) remember to wash hands after *every* diaper change
9) no wine before 4:00 PM
10) don't leave baby home alone to go buy cheddar cheese popcorn

DEAR BABY: Sorry,
I didn't realize you
could roll over.

DEAR BABY: Sorry at some point every day either my bra is undone or my shirt is open.

DEAR BABY: Sorry after spending four hours getting you to sleep via pacifier, swing, boob, bouncy seat, Bjorn, stroller, and six hundred laps on my shoulder, I sniffed and woke you up.

DEAR BABY: Sorry it looks like you don't know whether to go to Sunset Boulevard or clown school.

DEAR BABY: Sorry you couldn't see jack on our walk today.

DEAR BABY: Sorry but no amount of soap and hot water can save your precious "cuppy." My condolences.

DEAR BABY: Sorry we forgot your teething biscuits.

DEAR BABY: Sorry half your calories today came from dust bunnies.

DEAR BABY: Sorry tonight's wrestling match on the changing table ended with Desitin in your eye and a comb in your privates.

DEAR BABY: Sorry I forgot what I was wearing when I dressed you today.

DEAR BABY: Sorry you look like Mick Jagger and smell like a sewage plant.

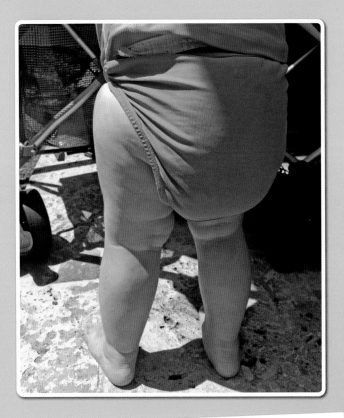

DEAR BABY: Sorry I didn't get the point of swim diapers. Until now.

DEAR BABY: Sorry we tried these on the day the pool closed.

DEAR BABY: Sorry I forgot to buy groceries and you had to eat blizzard for lunch.

DEAR BABY: Sorry, Momma needs a new pair of...anything. Just ONE thing that isn't for you.

DEAR BABY: Sorry you accidentally saw two dudes making meth instead of Elmo singing the alphabet.

That's Just Wrong

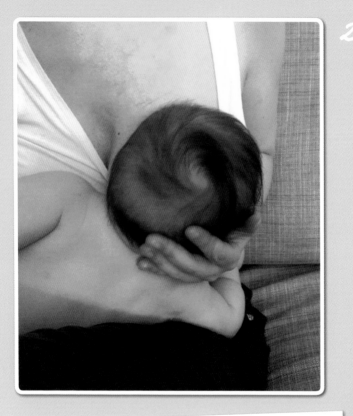

DEAR BABY: Sorry I wished you'd hurry the hell up and finish nursing so I could have a glass of Chardonnay.

DEAR BABY: Sorry but if you don't want to lie here, don't get so quiet every time you hear the bathroom fan.

DEAR BABY: Sorry I hated you for the first two weeks.

DEAR BABY: Sorry instead of thinking about you and your development I'm just wondering if my nipples will ever point up again.

DEAR BABY: Sorry I refer to your morning nap as "my first victory of the day."

DEAR BABY: Sorry, but the AARP called. They want their shorts back.

DEAR BABY: Sorry you saw the inside of a liquor store before 10:00 a.m.

DEAR BABY: Sorry I said you looked like Hannibal Lecter today.

DEAR BABY: Sorry I referred to the miracle of your birth as "Vaginageddon."

DEAR BABY: Sorry I opened up your diaper then closed it when I saw it was just pee.

DEAR BABY: Sorry I haven't taken you to the dentist yet because I *really* don't want to hear I have to brush your teeth twice a day.

DEAR BABY: Sorry I fantasized about sedating you today.

DEAR BABY: Sorry, so sorry, I saw this and said without thinking, "Oh, are you playing with Daddy's balls?"

DEAR BABY: Sorry I'm recording all your most precious moments on a bunch of Post-its and keeping them in a pencil cup next to the sink.

DEAR BABY: Sorry I dropped some Snoop on you today when I ran out of nursery rhymes.

DEAR BABY: Sorry I take Facebook personality quizzes on my phone when we're supposed to be bonding. (P.S. In case you're wondering, my animal soul mate is a tiny turtle on a skateboard.)

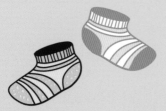

DEAR BABY: Sorry I just realized you're only awake for eight hours a day. Why does it feel like twenty?

DEAR BABY: Sorry I crammed you into this hot, itchy costume so I could post a pic showing everyone you're a cuter ladybug than their kid.

DEAR BABY: Sorry but it's time to clean up your *Law & Order: SVU* situation.

DEAR BABY: Sorry, but this beats wiping your rear end all day.

Mean Mommy

DEAR BABY: Sorry I took a photo instead of helping you up.

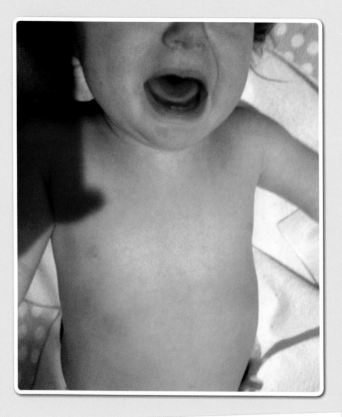

DEAR BABY: Sorry every time we put you on the changing table you think you're being shipped off to Guantanamo.

DEAR BABY: Sorry I so rudely suggested we wipe your nose.

DEAR BABY: Sorry I force you to hug me every day.

DEAR BABY: Sorry. You are not allowed to wake up yet.

DEAR BABY: Sorry. I'm going to stop now and save some for you, I swear.

DEAR BABY: Sorry, you may have the keys...but you still can't leave.

DEAR BABY: Sorry you have no say in when I publicly pick your nose.

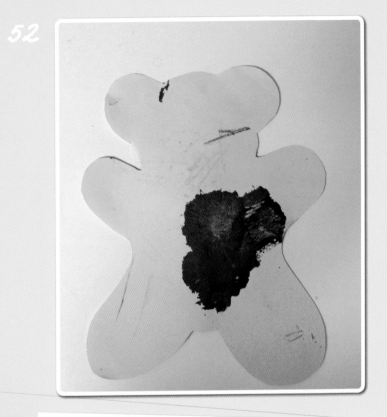

DEAR BABY: Sorry this "art" you made at "school" will not be making it to the fridge.

DEAR BABY: Sorry I made you pull an extra shift, but girl, my book club gets here in twenty.

DEAR BABY: Sorry, and enjoy, because this is as close as you're gonna get to having a puppy.

DEAR BABY: Sorry when you sweetly tried to share your food with me, I refused. I know where that hand has been.

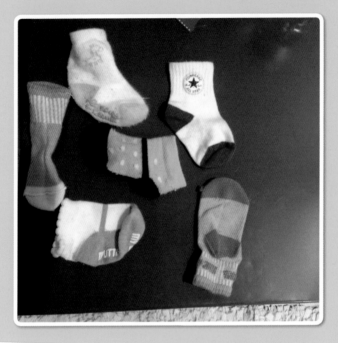

DEAR BABY: Sorry but I will not be trying to find where you dropped/hid each matching sock. These pairs are dead to me.

DEAR BABY: Sorry, you only have one chance to wear this hat before it goes back. Make it count.

DEAR BABY: Sorry, despite your whiny pleas to "do it self," I did not let you free-jump from the tip of your crib railing to the mattress below.

DEAR BABY: Sorry, but I'm not getting up from where I just sat down to push you. Make it work.

DEAR BABY: Sorry but this is payback for throwing up on me three times yesterday.

DEAR BABY: Sorry I zipped up your coat on a winter day.

DEAR BABY: Sorry, but there will be no tips for slow service.

DEAR BABY: Sorry about the trail of tears it took to make this hair vision a reality.

DEAR BABY: Sorry, you can't have the wine in this fridge. Now you know how I feel every day between lunch and your bedtime.

Daddy Knows Best?

DEAR BABY: Sorry Daddy doesn't realize a onesie is different than a shirt.

DEAR BABY: Sorry, but you got three rounds of patty-cake from Daddy before he had to take a nap. Consider yourself lucky.

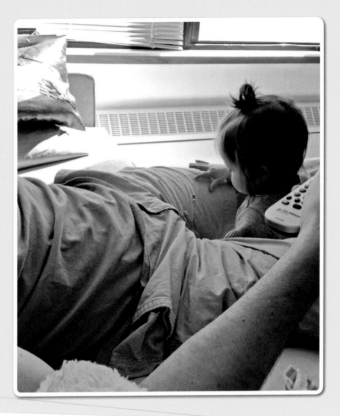

DEAR BABY: Sorry Daddy thought this was a good time to fart.

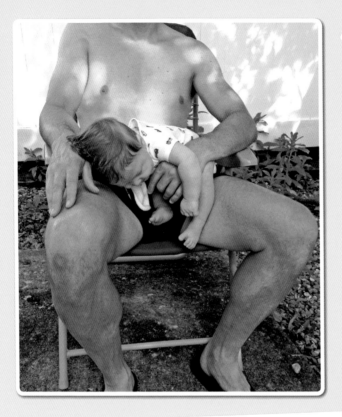

DEAR BABY: Sorry this is Daddy's version of tummy time.

DEAR BABY: Sorry daddy thought it was appropriate to let you snuggle up on the couch for a program called "Hitler's Suicide Ship."

DEAR BABY: Sorry when I squinted across the room at you and Daddy sweetly sitting next to each other and asked what you were holding in your mouth he said, "Just a screwdriver."

DEAR BABY: Sorry Daddy called your baby sling a "strap on."

DEAR BABY: Sorry Daddy thought that because "it was a hard poo" he could leave it in your diaper until bedtime—three hours from now.

DEAR BABY: Sorry Daddy has no idea how a barrette works.

My resolution is to get healthier while still destroying myself with alcohol and drugs.

DEAR BABY: Sorry Daddy doesn't realize this shirt loses its humor at day care pickup.

DEAR BABY: Sorry Daddy didn't get the memo that baby shoes are in fact meant for specific feet.

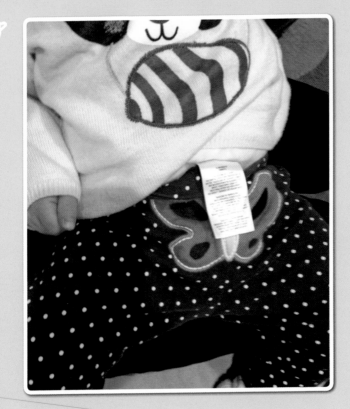

DEAR BABY: Sorry Daddy suffers from a mysterious disease called "Can't See Tags for Shit."

Lazy Parenting
101

DEAR BABY: Sorry this has been out here so long you think it's your closet.

DEAR BABY: Sorry I put you in the ExerSaucer for an hour so I could try on shoes with different outfits.

DEAR BABY: Sorry the only time I wash your toys anymore is when they get run over in the street.

DEAR BABY: Sorry we're too lazy to get you your own coat.

DEAR BABY: Sorry so much of your life is lying around, staring into space. Wait a minute, that sounds awesome. #sorrynotsorry

DEAR BABY: Sorry this evening's pre-bedtime entertainment was me crunching chips in your face.

DEAR BABY: Sorry this is your new home for two hours every day while Mommy takes long showers and texts everyone she knows from the gym locker room.

DEAR BABY: Sorry I pretended not to see (or smell) the giant turd in your diaper so Daddy would have to deal with it.

DEAR BABY: Sorry these are today's featured new toys.

DEAR BABY: Sorry, it's easier to put you in a snowsuit than clean the floor.

DEAR BABY: Sorry, just trying to keep it real on Take Your Child to Work Day.

DEAR BABY: Sorry today's playdate is with any random who will talk to you in the car inspection waiting room.

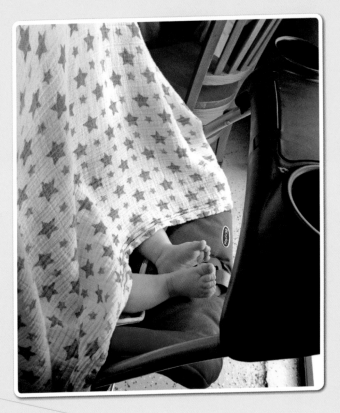

DEAR BABY: Sorry half your life is me carting you to coffee shops under a shroud and praying your feet don't move.

DEAR BABY: Sorry but I need a night off. Milk's in the fridge, *Mickey Mouse Clubhouse* marathon on TV. Have fun.

DEAR BABY: Sorry, that diaper blowout was about two hours too close to bedtime for a wardrobe change.

DEAR BABY: Sorry this Fourth of July weekend we celebrated our freedom to do bath time in various backyard pools.

DEAR BABY: Sorry I left this by the door long enough for you to use it as a bench.

A Moment's Peace. The Struggle is <u>Real.</u>

DEAR BABY: Sorry
I shut this so I could
tweeze in peace.

DEAR BABY: Sorry this is where you'll be hanging out until the baby gate arrives.

DEAR BABY: Sorry I told Daddy I had a fake errand so I could relax in a corner of West Elm with a bag of Doritos.

DEAR BABY: Sorry when I don't know what to do with you I just hold you up to the pantry to look at spices.

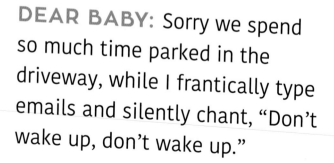

DEAR BABY: Sorry we spend so much time parked in the driveway, while I frantically type emails and silently chant, "Don't wake up, don't wake up."

DEAR BABY: Sorry the whole time you were narrating the pretend "fruit salad" you were making out of blocks, I was brainstorming reasons to go to Target.

DEAR BABY: Sorry I said there were Cheerios in there so I could have two minutes alone.

DEAR BABY: Sorry it might be a while before you find *The Nose Book*, which we have read six million times, because it somehow got thrown in the back of my closet.

DEAR BABY: Sorry my parting words when Daddy took you out today were: "Don't rush back."

DEAR BABY: Sorry I've only just discovered the ultimate "keep you quiet while I make dinner" activity—playing a computer slide show of your favorite subject: you.

DEAR BABY: Sorry when you and Daddy came downstairs looking for me and I was on the toilet, I suddenly lost my voice... and accidentally locked the door.

DEAR BABY: Sorry I brought my smoothie into the bathroom so I could drink it all myself.

DEAR BABY: Sorry I lied and said this was broken so I wouldn't have to lift and hold your ass up for the longest sip ever.

I Should Probably Care More

DEAR BABY: Sorry I binge-watched five seasons of *Game of Thrones* instead of reading that Baby Whisperer book.

DEAR BABY: Sorry this is my "system" for remembering to periodically bathe.

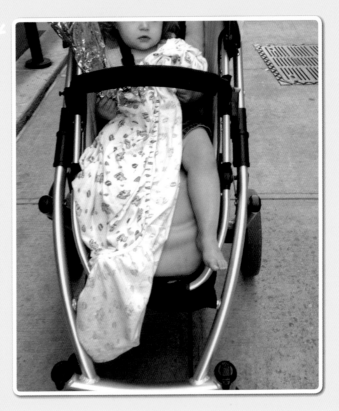

DEAR BABY: Sorry I let you roll outside like a hobo.

DEAR BABY: Sorry you've learned at such a tender young age to say "Oh shit" in proper context when things don't go your way. (P.S. Proud of you.)

DEAR BABY: Sorry I put you to bed knowing full well you had avocado in your hair.

DEAR BABY: Sorry I am your role model of femininity and THIS is my uniform.

DEAR BABY: Sorry I pretended not to hear that liquid fart right after I put you in a fresh diaper.

DEAR BABY: Sorry the scent you're learning to associate with me is body odor and stale coffee.

DEAR BABY: Sorry this is what qualifies as "baby-proofing" in our house.

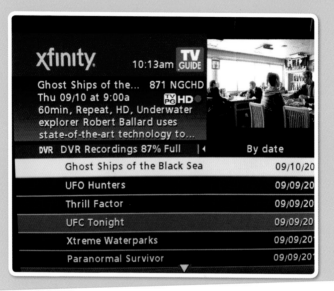

DEAR BABY: Sorry I spent half your awake time figuring out which of Daddy's ridiculous shows I could delete without him noticing.

DEAR BABY: Sorry you are basically our Swiffer.

Technically Not My Fault But...

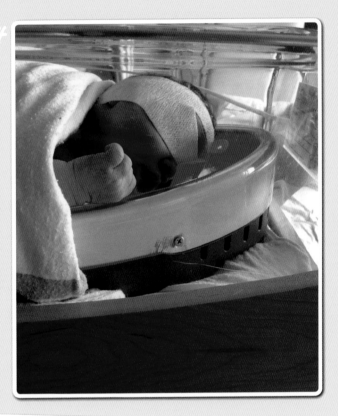

DEAR BABY: Sorry you thought you were traveling to freedom but instead you ended up blindfolded in a tanning bed.

DEAR BABY: Sorry. Next time, don't sleep through lunch.

DEAR BABY: Sorry it will take hundreds of dollars in yoga classes later to do the move you're doing right now for free.

DEAR BABY: Sorry you had to spend ten minutes rolling on the ground to behold some holiday splendor.

DEAR BABY: Sorry you had to watch us eat delicious bacon when all you get is the same watered-down beverage at every meal.

DEAR BABY: Sorry though you can sleep while belted into an open-air object, rolling along a pothole-infested road next to a passing train, the sound of me opening this bag next to your room disturbed your delicate slumber.

DEAR BABY: Sorry you're not feeling well and thanks for sneezing in my mouth like three times today.

DEAR BABY: Sorry you don't know yet that your thumb-sucking hand should not also be your "down your pants" hand.

DEAR BABY: Sorry, but if you "use potty" as you claim, why did I just find a dump in your diaper?

DEAR BABY: Sorry, but we may need to revoke your "me do it!" privileges.

DEAR BABY: Sorry, you cannot kiss every single card with a doggy on it.

DEAR BABY: Sorry, but I hope this isn't the start of a career of staying past last call.

DEAR BABY: Sorry there's no one to play with because you brought us here at the ass crack of dawn.

DEAR BABY: Sorry, "Funny-heena" is not the name of any book, anywhere in this country. Now, *Thumbelina*...that is a classic.

DEAR BABY: Sorry you got taken down during that goodbye hug.

DEAR BABY: Sorry you "no like it, pants" but I "no like" putting the kid from *The Exorcist* in a car seat every day. So, we're even.

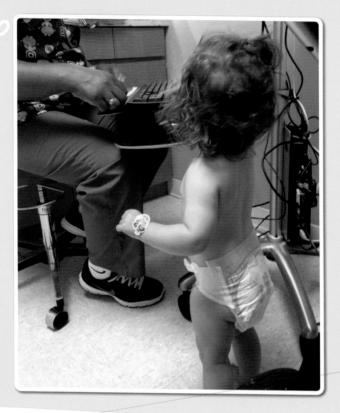

DEAR BABY: Sorry, but saying you got two polio shots won't get you an extra sticker.

DEAR BABY: Sorry you are so worn out from all that napping and snacking.

DEAR BABY: Sorry it's totally sunny outside.

DEAR BABY: Sorry you decided to poop directly into your floor vent and now your room is going to smell like a hot turd the rest of winter.

DEAR BABY: Sorry Mr. Squirrel won't share his food with you. It's called karma.

DEAR BABY: Sorry I can't play with you because I'm busy chopping all your food into f&#%g 1×1 centimeter chunks.

DEAR BABY: Sorry, did one of these five men wielding motorized equipment ten feet from your room disturb your nap?

The Truth Hurts

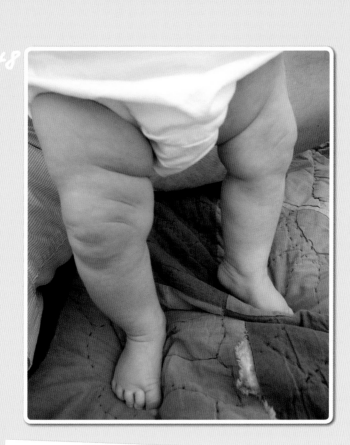

DEAR BABY: Sorry, but I don't think "leg model" is in your future.

DEAR BABY: Sorry you'll need a second mortgage for all the product this is gonna take.

DEAR BABY: Sorry but the goal of this trip is relaxation. You are not invited.

DEAR BABY: Sorry, but if you're going to make it as a career girl you have to stop drinking from the humidifier.

DEAR BABY: Sorry one of my favorite things is when you are locked into the backseat for a good twenty-minute drive.

DEAR BABY: Sorry the best part of my day was when you were melting down and I saw a beer in the fridge and remembered I could drink.

DEAR BABY: Sorry you are genetically destined for a cupcake addiction.

DEAR BABY: Sorry no one will ever be as good-looking...as you are to yourself.

Grilled Pound Cake
Ice Cream Sandwich

DEAR BABY: Sorry we left you home alone with a stranger to come eat this.

DEAR BABY: Sorry, you're not going to find anything down there for a long time. (And when you do, it won't be much.)

DEAR BABY: Sorry I "forgot" to outline the terms of your vacation contract. Phase One: four hours as carry-on luggage. You shall have two square feet to play, eat, sleep, and poo.

DEAR BABY: Sorry I find you the cutest when I haven't seen you in a few hours.

DEAR BABY: Sorry instead of gazing lovingly at your face while you nurse, I'm just counting all the lint, dirt, and crumbs on the floor I have to pick up as soon as you're done.

DEAR BABY: Sorry, but I'm missing the good old days when I could put you in your high chair with some oatmeal and it would be a half hour before you wanted to get down.

DEAR BABY: Sorry I timed how long it was after you woke up before you cried about nothing. It was fifty-seven seconds. Try harder.

And Then There's...

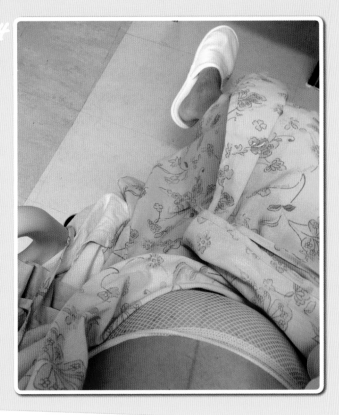

DEAR BABY: Sorry my hospital outfit gave you the impression I only had a few years left.

MUM seeks sun hat baby will not be able to remove from head.
Married, unshowered mom seeks sun hat child will not be able to rip from gourd and toss violently to ground. Must have SPF and military-strength cord w/plastic do-hickey you can squeeze to cinch hat within an inch of cutting off child's air supply under chin. No cute cotton ties or Velcro chin straps. (Girl, please. That shit would be thrown in a ditch every five seconds.) Please, tell me where this mythical creation can be found! Seeking LTR, but will settle for just a few weeks until we lose it.

© Dear Baby XO

DEAR BABY: Sorry, I'm trying to find you a hat that will stay on during the Apocalypse.

DEAR BABY: Sorry when I ran out of indoor activities, I took you to Macy's to run the aisles with a string cheese.

DEAR BABY: Sorry I used St. Patrick's Day as an opportunity to dress you like a leprechaun even though you're only one-sixteenth, possibly one-eighth Irish.

DEAR BABY: Sorry you are descended from hoarders.

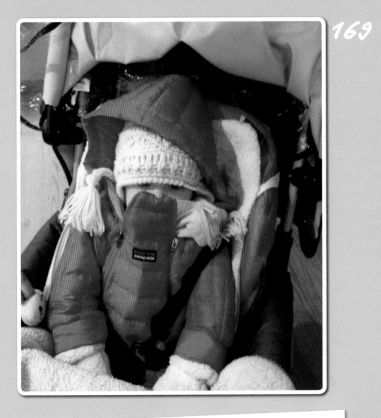

DEAR BABY: Sorry you look like Randy from *A Christmas Story*.

DEAR BABY: Sorry we ran out of animal crackers right before your mall walkathon.

DEAR BABY: Sorry I had to pull last night's broccoli out of your neck folds today.

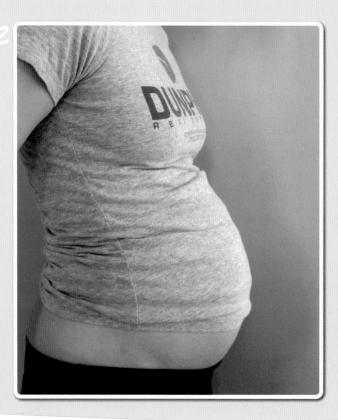

DEAR BABY: Sorry...but you are about to be dethroned.

ACKNOWLEDGMENTS

Thank you to my husband for encouraging this and all my ideas, being 100% willing to be the butt of the joke and listening to me recite endless rearrangements of the same ten words.

Thanks to all the badass mama bloggers who let me see it was possible to be an overwhelmed mom and build something at the same time.

Thanks to Matt McGowan at Frances Goldin for seeing the potential and Shana Drehs at Sourcebooks for enthusiastically transforming *Dear Baby XO* from a Facebook page into this book.

Thanks to the awesome *Dear Baby XO* online readers for your comments and participation. You make confessing my parenting fails on the Internet fun.

To my sweet babies. For being an endless source of material.

And to my mom, for saying funny, un-PC things about parenting before it was cool. I wish you could read this.

ABOUT THE AUTHOR

Photo courtesy of Deirdre Herlihy

In addition to being a pro bono toddler personal chef, chauffeur and dry cleaner, **Sarah Showfety** is a writer whose work has been featured in *Today Parents*, the *Huffington Post*, *ABC News*, *Buzzfeed*, the *New York Post*, *Yahoo!*, the *Daily Mail*, and other publications. She has appeared on *The Doctors*, *The Better Show*, and *The Lisa Oz Show*. She is the creator of the popular blog *Dear Baby XO* and the humorous web series *Pregnancy 411: Stuff You Need to Know if You Have a Fetus.*

dearbabyxo.com
facebook.com/dearbabyxo